GLORY

THE STRUGGLE FOR YARDS

RALPH BROOKS
AND
GARY BURLEY

iUniverse®

GLORY
THE STRUGGLE FOR YARDS

iUniverse books may be ordered through booksellers or by contacting:

iUniverse
1663 Liberty Drive
Bloomington, IN 47403
www.iuniverse.com
844-349-9409

ISBN: 978-1-6632-2838-3 (sc)
ISBN: 978-1-6632-2839-0 (e)

Library of Congress Control Number: 2021918704

Print information available on the last page.

iUniverse rev. date: 08/27/2021

CONTENTS

DEDICATION

This book is dedicated to my wife, Bobbie Burley. She was elected as the fifteenth president; and First African-American Female to hold that honor at Miles College. I was able to play in the NFL league for ten years amongst other great veterans. I chased quarterbacks all over the field but learned the fastest way to the quarterback is running in a straight line. What can I say, to the love of my life, my best friend and favorite first lady who has been by side through cancer recovery and never allowed me to let go of my faith in God and his unchanging hands. She is my rock through difficult surgeries and ongoing health issues. While taking care of me, she still found a way for 37 years to keep the lights on for the people in Birmingham, Alabama before retiring in 2016 as Vice President of Alabama Power Company. This book is a gift of gratitude, respect, admiration and praiseworthy to my wife, who means the world to me.

Gary Burley (left) and Bobbie Burley (Right)

FOREWORD

This amazing book is all about unknown stories of the African American Pioneers that have paved the way for both past & present NFL Players. This journey you will have the opportunity to experience without putting on the shoulder pads. I've been a Big fan of Football since playing as a kid, but after getting hit & broken up a few times, I realized I need to play music instead. Lol, Football is a reflection of Hard Knocks Life. My friend, Gary Burley not only talked the talk, he also walked the walk. Read all about it right here, right now.

–Bootsy Baby!!!

Gary Burley (Right) and Bootsy Collins (Left)

ACKNOWLEDGEMENT

In memories of the late, Dave Smith of the (Pittsburgh Steeler), who had been working on this idea of writing a book with Gary Burly before he got sick and passed away. We want to acknowledge him and wish he were here to witness the making of Glory, "The Struggle for Yards. We want to recognize the Players, Owners and Commissioner of the NFL both in present and past times. And also great appreciation to Valencia Belle, ACT Certified Educator of Schools/Cleared programs. In addition, a special thank goes to Charles Barkley, for supporting this vision of the untold stories of the forgotten legends in the NFL.

Gary Burley (left) Charles Barkley (Right)

"People who are successful live in the present and the moment and not the future but the most important thing is to learn from the past lessons".

–Charles Barkley

ADDITIONAL ACKNOWLEDGEMENT

I would like to thank Ellie Go my check in coordinator and Reed Samuel from iUniverse for helping me with this project.

Darlene A. and Mac Greco thank you for
your support and guidance.

INTRODUCTION

The National Football League (NFL) was founded in 1920 in Canton, Ohio, as the American Professional Football Association. The first president was Jim Thorpe, an outstanding American athlete who played against Fritz Pollard. On June 24, 1922. The American Professional officially renames itself the National Football League. Glory talks about the compelling stories of the forgotten legends and their early life, college careers, professional football, later years and legacy of the post area of the National Football League (NFL). Some of the many great stories you will find in this book, Fritz Pollard, The first black head coach in the NFL and playing running back at the same time for the undefeated Akron Pros in 1920. In 1946, The Los Angeles Rams sign Kenny Washington and Woody Strode, who will become the first African- Americans to play in the NFL in the modern era, ending 12 years drought from 1934 to 1946 where there were no black players playing in the NFL during this period.

Gary Burley believes these stories must be acknowledged and written, Glory is important and should be in the local public and private schools, black colleges, libraries, universities, communities and athletic venues as an educational guidance, says, Burley. We are living in the now (present) time and making our own history but the past-history of the NL players lives is still valuable today for everyone to learn from their struggles during their area. We have to understand that history continues to shape our relationship between societies and peoples of all races based on the choices we make in life. Gary Burley (former NFL player for the Cincinnati Bengal and Atlanta Falcons) vision of this book is to teach others the culture and roots of the past and present pioneers players in the NFL. Glory is a journey of unforgotten legends struggle for yards through changes of values, philosophy, beliefs and principles. Finally, we leave you with a branch of knowledge, facts and awareness that explains and records past events of some of the first NFL Greatest Players of all Times.

AUTHOR NOTES

The book, Glory: The Struggle for Yards are stories gathered together to illustrate the unique cultures, history and values that unite people of all races together. It is so much more than a book of facts and individual's personal accomplishments. Glory share stories that include powerful messages that can inspire, teach, and influence others to achieve their goals in life. These stories bring facts to life and have the ability to connect the past with the present. We start with diversity and inclusion by respecting, understanding and appreciating each other's humanities and beliefs and most of all reading to know for your own gratification and personal experiences. These stories promote a positive attitude through football legends hardships, fears and never losing desire for taking care of their families and leaving a legacy for the future generation to understand their challenges, difficulties, misfortune and adversities.

We have to remember before writing books, ancestors told stories by cave painting on the wall, as they would blow the paint through hollow bones very similar to today's airbrushing. Campfires was also a form of storytelling performed around an open fire at night and mostly in the wilderness. We see it in today modern campfires stories with Girls Scouts and Boy Scouts of America and even with good old family reunion barbecue in the front or backyard. Glory is a book of legendary football stories that helps us understand our differences in culture with other peoples so that we can connect and communicate in love and make new friends through story telling.

GAME TIME

First African-American official in the NFL

We wanted to start the book out with this amazing story about Burl Abron Toler Sr. Burl Abron Toler was born in Memphis on May 9, 1928. His mother, Annie King Toler, operated a small store and ran a boarding house. His father, Arnold, was a Pullman porter (men hired to work on the railroads as porters). Burl Toler went to a segregated high school and he did not get a chance to play football in high school. He had an accident with cooking grease that left a severe burn on his arm. Burl graduated from high school and went on to San Francisco to where his uncle lived. He enrolled at City College in San Francisco to attend for two years. The football coach spotted him in the gym and asked him to try out for the football team. Ollie Matson was the star running back. Burl playing the linebacker position tackled Ollie on three consecutive plays during his first day at practice. He and Ollie Matson lead their team to the 1948 Mythical Junior College National Championship. He was a member of the 1951 undefeated Dons football team. The Dons appeared destined for a bowl game that would have provided the university with much-needed funds to keep the football program afloat. After capping a 9-0 regular season with a 20-2 victory over Loyola at the Rose bowl, USF received a conditional invitation to the Orange Bowl.

The Greatest act of brotherly Love

What are we talking about? What are the condition to the invitation? The condition were that Matson and Toler, the two Black players, would not be allowed to play in the game. The team agreed that there were nothing, really, to talk about. The Dons football team declined the invitation. They believed that the team was a team and member would be excluded because the color of their skin. The late Bob St. Clair said at a 2011 event to commemorate the 60- year anniversary of the team, "We told them to go to hell." That was the end of the football season because the team was not going without Ollie and Burl. The team could have played for the money to keep the football program going but they choose respect and compassion that will go down in history with them for the rest of their lives.

Burl Toler was an American football official in the National League (NFL) from 1965 until 1989.

CHAPTER ONE

Early Years Pre-NFL

First Black Professional American Football Player

Charles W. Follis was born on February 3, 1879 to James Henry and Catherine Matilda Anderson Follis in Cloverdale, Virginia. He was the first Black professional American football player. He played for the Shelby Blues of the "Ohio League" from 1902 to 1906. Follis signed a contract on September 16, 1904, with Shelby Blues making him the first Black man contracted to play professional football on an integrated team. Charles Follies life story were featured in a play called the Black Cyclone at Mansfield Senior High School in Ohio. The play was about the historical pioneer, Charles Follis, the First African American Pro Football Player. He was also the first Black catcher to move from college baseball into the Negro Leagues. Charles Follis developed pneumonia at the early age of 31 and died on April 5, 1910. He is buried in Wooster Cemetery in Wooster, Ohio, where he went to high school and college.

CHAPTER TWO

Early Years Pre-NFL

Second Black Professional American Football Player

Charles "Doc" Baker was a very interesting man starting with no records for the day that he was born. He was raised in the Akron Children's Home, an orphanage in Akron, Ohio. There is very little known about his life outside of football. He was the second-ever African American to play professional football, the first being Charles Follis and how ironic they both had the same first name. He played for the Akron Indians of the "Ohio League" from 1906-1908. In 1911, he returned to the team for one last season. I know you are probably wondering about his middle name "Doc" and where did it come from? Charles "Doc" Baker earned his nickname, "Doc", while serving as an aide to a physician in Akron, Ohio. I was not able to find the college he attended or the burial place for Charles "Doc" Baker. My understanding through reading is that he died in the early 1920s.

CHAPTER THREE

Early Years Pre-NFL

Black Professional American Football Player

Henry McDonald was born on August 31, 1890 in Port-au-Prince, Hati. His parents agreed to allow their son to be adopted by his father employer, an American banana and coconut importer. Henry McDonald spoke about his parents decision and being thankful for the opportunity for him to grow up in the United States. He took his family back to Haiti for visit after not seeing his mother in 55 years. McDonald spent his early childhood days in Canandaigua, New York before his family later moved to Rochester. There he became the first black American to graduate from Rochester's East High School.

In 1911, McDonald began playing professional football for the Oxford Pros. McDonald played halfback in his first professional game against the Rochester Jeffersons. Leo Lyons was the owner and coach of the Rochester Jeffersons. Lyons promptly enticed him to play for his team after being amazed by McDonald's speed. He was named the nickname "Motorcycle McDonald" because of his ability to run so fast. The world record at the time for running 100 yards was 10 flat. According to McDonald, he could run a 100 yards in 10.2 seconds.

Throughout his professional career, McDonald had a hard time making ends meet by playing football. He never took home more than $15 a day and to brought that amount home he had to play two games. He would take a trolley to Canandaigua to play for the town team in the afternoon and he played the morning game in Rochester for the Jeffersons. McDonald only mention one negative racial incident during his 7 seasons of playing professional football. In 1917, Greasy Neale, who played for the Canton Bulldogs, coached by the legendary Jim Thrope. He threw McDonald out of bounds and said, "Black is black and White is white and where I come from the two don't mix." McDonald was a boxer so quite naturally he was ready to fight Neale. Jim Thrope intervened and stated to Neale, We are here to play football.

In 1990 Henry McDonald was inducted in the inaugural class of the Geneva New York Sports Hall of Fame. McDonald was a charter member of the Black Athlete's Hall of Fame, along with Jackie Robinson, Jim Brown and Willie Mays. In 1937 Henry McDonald was named the head football coach at DeSales High School. This made him the first black American to serve as a high school coach in New York State. He was the team coach until 1943. According to The New York Times Archives, Henry McDonald died at Geneva General Hospital, where he had been admitted recently for hip surgery. He was 85 years old. He died on June 12, 1976.

CHAPTER FOUR

Early Years Pre-NFL

First African-American varsity athlete in any sport at MAC

Gideon Edward Smith was an American Coach and Football player. He was born on July 13, 1889 in Lansing, Michigan. He was sometimes referred to as G.E. Smith. He played college football at Michigan Agricultural College (MAC), now known as Michigan State University, from 1913 to 1915. Smith served as a teacher in 1920 at the Virginia State College. In 1921, Smith became the head football coach at Hampton Institute, now known as Hampton University, in Hampton, Virginia. Smith died on May 6, 1968, at Veterans Hospital in Salem Virginia, following a long illness.

CHAPTER FIVE

Early Years Pre-NFL

Fredrick Douglas Pollard was born in an wealthy neighborhood in Chicago on January 27, 1894, to John William, a barber, and Catherine Amanda Hughs Pollard, a seamstress. He was the seventh of eight children; they called him Fred, but later the nickname "Fritz" came by the residents in the neighborhood, a name that stuck with him throughout life.

What high school did Fritz Pollard attend?

Pollard attended Albert G. Lane Manual Training High School in Chicago, also known as "Lane Tech," where he played football, baseball, and ran track. Lane Tech College Prep High School is a public 4-year selective enrollment magnet high school located in the Roscoe Village neighborhood on the north side of Chicago. The school is named after Albert G. Lane, a former superintendent and principal of Chicago Public Schools from 1891 until 1898. It was founded in 1908 and dedicated on Washington Birthday in 1909, as the Albert Grannis Lane Manual Training High School.

The school was a manual training for boys, where students could take advantage of a wide array of technical classes. Freshman were offered wood turning, cabinet making, and carpentry.

Sophomores received training in welding, molding, forge, foundry and coremaking. Juniors could take classes in the machine shop. Seniors were able to take electric shop which was the most advanced shop course. In 1971, there were changes made to the admission policy due to drop in enrollment and the lack of technical schools for girls. James Redmond, the school Superintendent recommended that girls be admitted to Lane Tech. The Chicago Board of Education agreed and for the first time girls were able to enroll at Lane Tech.

What University did Fritz Pollard go too?

First Black Football Player at Brown University

Fritz went to Brown University and he majored in chemistry. Brown University is a private Ivy League research university in Providence, Rhode Island. Fritz was one of the greatest running back who ever lived. He was one of the earliest pioneers of football. Fritz Pollard was a 5-9, 165-pound running back out of Brown University. He had the tenacity of Walter "Sweetness" Payton, the intangibility and elusiveness of Barry Sanders and the quickness and speed of Tony Dorsett. He played three positions, Quarterback, Running back and Halfback at Brown University.

Fritz had to win over his teammates. He went through so much to be a football player for Brown University. He was so great that he made a way out of no way when others would have quitted. He paved the way for the African Americans that we currently see in the NFL today.

What bowl game did Fritz Pollard play in for Brown University?

First Black Football Player at Brown University to play in the Rose Bowl

Fritz Pollard played halfback on the Brown football team, which went to the 1916 Rose Bowl also known as "The Granddaddy of Them All", because it is the oldest bowl game. He was the first black football player from Brown University to play in the Rose Bowl.

The Rose Bowl Game is an annual American college football game, usually played on January 1 (New Year's Day at the Rose Bowl in the Los Angeles suburb of Pasadena, California. The Rose Bowl was first played in 1902 as the Tournament East-West football game, and has been played annually since 1916. Before the Rose Bowl was built, games were played in Pasadena's Tournament Park, approximately three miles southeast of the current Rose Bowl stadium, near the campus of Caltech.

Rose Bowls games from January 1, 1902 until January 1, 2021

Winners appear in boldface

Date played	West / Pac-12		East / Big Ten		Attendance[60]	Notes
January 1, 1902	Stanford	0	**Michigan**	49	8,000	notes
January 1, 1916	**Washington State**	14	Brown	0	7,000	notes
January 1, 1917	**Oregon**	14	Penn	0	26,000	notes
January 1, 1918[c]	**Mare Island – USMC**	19	Camp Lewis – US Army	7	N/A	notes
January 1, 1919[c]	Mare Island – USMC	0	**Great Lakes – US Navy**	17	N/A	notes
January 1, 1920	Oregon	6	**Harvard**	7	30,000	notes
January 1, 1921	**California**	28	Ohio State	0	42,000	notes
January 2, 1922	*California*	0	*Washington & Jefferson*	0	40,000	notes
January 1, 1923	**USC**	14	Penn State	3	43,000	notes
January 1, 1924	*Washington*	14	*Navy*	14	40,000	notes
January 1, 1925	Stanford	10	**Notre Dame**	27	53,000	notes
January 1, 1926	Washington	19	**Alabama**	20	50,000	notes
January 1, 1927	*Stanford*	7	*Alabama*	7	57,417	notes
January 2, 1928	**Stanford**	7	Pittsburgh	6	65,000	notes
January 1, 1929	California	7	**Georgia Tech**	8	66,604	notes
January 1, 1930	**USC**	47	Pittsburgh	14	72,000	notes
January 1, 1931	Washington State	0	**Alabama**	24	60,000	notes
January 1, 1932	**USC**	21	Tulane	12	75,562	notes
January 2, 1933	**USC**	35	Pittsburgh	0	78,874	notes
January 1, 1934	Stanford	0	**Columbia**	7	35,000	notes
January 1, 1935	Stanford	13	**Alabama**	29	84,474	notes
January 1, 1936	**Stanford**	7	SMU	0	84,474	notes
January 1, 1937	#5 Washington	0	**#3 Pittsburgh**	21	87,196	notes
January 1, 1938	**#2 California**	13	#4 Alabama	0	90,000	notes
January 2, 1939	**#7 USC**	7	#3 Duke	3	89,452	notes
January 1, 1940	**#3 USC**	14	#2 Tennessee	0	92,200	notes
January 1, 1941	**#2 Stanford**	21	#7 Nebraska	13	91,500	notes
January 1, 1942	**#12 Oregon State**	20	#2 Duke	16	56,000[a]	notes
January 1, 1943	#13 UCLA	0	**#2 Georgia**	9	93,000	notes
January 1, 1944	**USC**	29	#12 Washington	0	68,000	notes
January 1, 1945	**#7 USC**	25	#12 Tennessee	0	91,000	notes
January 1, 1946	#11 USC	14	**#2 Alabama**	34	93,000	notes
January 1, 1947	#4 UCLA	14	**#5 Illinois**	45	90,000	notes

Date played	West / Pac-12		East / Big Ten		Attendance[60]	Notes
January 1, 1948	#8 USC	0	#2 **Michigan**	49	93,000	notes
January 1, 1949	#4 California	14	#7 **Northwestern**	20	93,000	notes
January 2, 1950	#3 California	14	#6 **Ohio State**	17	100,963	notes
January 1, 1951	#5 California	6	#9 **Michigan**	14	98,939	notes
January 1, 1952	#7 Stanford	7	#4 **Illinois**	40	96,825	notes
January 1, 1953	#5 **USC**	7	#11 Wisconsin	0	101,500	notes
January 1, 1954	#5 UCLA	20	#3 **Michigan State**	28	101,000	notes
January 1, 1955	#17 USC	7	#1 **Ohio State**	20	89,191	notes
January 2, 1956	#4 UCLA	14	#2 **Michigan State**	17	100,809	notes
January 1, 1957	#10 Oregon State	19	#3 **Iowa**	35	97,126	notes
January 1, 1958	Oregon	7	#2 **Ohio State**	10	98,202	notes
January 1, 1959	#16 California	12	#2 **Iowa**	38	98,297	notes
January 1, 1960	#8 **Washington**	44	#6 Wisconsin	8	100,809	notes
January 2, 1961	#6 **Washington**	17	#1 Minnesota	7	97,314	notes
January 1, 1962	#16 UCLA	3	#6 **Minnesota**	21	98,214	notes
January 1, 1963	#1 **USC**	42	#2 Wisconsin	37	98,698	notes
January 1, 1964	Washington	7	#3 **Illinois**	17	96,957	notes
January 1, 1965	#8 Oregon State	7	#4 **Michigan**	34	100,423	notes
January 1, 1966	#5 **UCLA**	14	#1 Michigan State	12	100,087	notes
January 2, 1967	USC	13	#7 **Purdue**	14	100,807	notes
January 1, 1968	#1 **USC**	14	#4 Indiana	3	102,946	notes
January 1, 1969	#2 USC	16	#1 **Ohio State**	27	102,063	notes
January 1, 1970	#5 **USC**	10	#7 Michigan	3	103,878	notes
January 1, 1971	#12 **Stanford**	27	#2 Ohio State	17	103,839	notes
January 1, 1972	#16 **Stanford**	13	#4 Michigan	12	103,154	notes
January 1, 1973	#1 **USC**	42	#3 Ohio State	17	106,869	notes
January 1, 1974	#7 USC	21	#4 **Ohio State**	42	105,267	notes
January 1, 1975	#5 **USC**	18	#3 Ohio State	17	106,721	notes
January 1, 1976	#11 **UCLA**	23	#1 Ohio State	10	105,464	notes
January 1, 1977	#3 **USC**	14	#2 Michigan	6	106,182	notes
January 2, 1978	#13 **Washington**	27	#4 Michigan	20	105,312	notes
January 1, 1979	#3 **USC**	17	#5 Michigan	10	105,629	notes
January 1, 1980	#3 **USC**	17	#1 Ohio State	16	105,526	notes
January 1, 1981	#16 Washington	6	#5 **Michigan**	23	104,863	notes
January 1, 1982	#12 **Washington**	28	#13 Iowa	0	105,611	notes
January 1, 1983	#5 **UCLA**	24	#19 Michigan	14	104,991	notes
January 2, 1984	**UCLA**	45	#4 Illinois	9	103,217	notes
January 1, 1985	#18 USC	20	#6 Ohio State	17	102,594	notes

11

Date played	West / Pac-12	East / Big Ten	Attendance[60]	Notes
January 1, 1986	#13 **UCLA**	45 #4 Iowa	28 103,292	notes
January 1, 1987	#7 **Arizona State**	22 #4 Michigan	15 103,168	notes
January 1, 1988	#16 USC	17 #8 **Michigan State**	20 103,847	notes
January 2, 1989	#5 USC	14 #11 **Michigan**	22 101,688	notes
January 1, 1990	#12 **USC**	17 #3 Michigan	10 103,450	notes
January 1, 1991	#8 **Washington**	46 #17 Iowa	34 101,273	notes
January 1, 1992	#2 **Washington**	34 #4 Michigan	14 103,566	notes
January 1, 1993	#9 Washington	31 #7 **Michigan**	38 94,236	notes
January 1, 1994	#14 UCLA	16 #9 **Wisconsin**	21 101,237	notes
January 2, 1995	#12 Oregon	20 #2 **Penn State**	38 102,247	notes
January 1, 1996	#17 **USC**	41 #3 Northwestern	32 100,102	notes
January 1, 1997	#2 Arizona State	17 #4 **Ohio State**	20 100,635	notes
January 1, 1998	#8 Washington State	16 #1 **Michigan**	21 101,219	notes
January 1, 1999	#6 UCLA	31 #9 **Wisconsin**	38 93,872	notes
January 1, 2000	#22 Stanford	9 #4 **Wisconsin**	17 93,731	notes
January 1, 2001	#4 **Washington**	34 #14 Purdue	24 94,392	notes
January 3, 2002[d]	#4 Nebraska	14 #1 **Miami (FL)**	37 93,781	notes
January 1, 2003	#7 Washington State	14 #8 **Oklahoma**	34 86,848	notes
January 1, 2004	#1 **USC**	28 #4 Michigan	14 93,849	notes
January 1, 2005	#6 **Texas**	38 #13 Michigan	37 93,468	notes
January 4, 2006[d]	#1 USC	38 #2 **Texas**	41 93,986	notes
January 1, 2007	#8 **USC**	32 #3 Michigan	18 93,852	notes
January 1, 2008	#6 **USC**	49 #13 Illinois	17 93,923	notes
January 1, 2009	#5 **USC**	38 #6 Penn State	24 93,293	notes
January 1, 2010	#7 Oregon	17 #8 **Ohio State**	26 93,963	notes
January 1, 2011	#3 **TCU**	21 #4 Wisconsin	19 94,118	notes
January 2, 2012	#6 **Oregon**	45 #9 Wisconsin	38 91,245	notes
January 1, 2013	#8 **Stanford**	20 #23 Wisconsin	14 93,359	notes
January 1, 2014	#5 Stanford	20 #4 **Michigan State**	24 95,173	notes
January 1, 2015[e]	#3 **Oregon**	59 #2 Florida State	20 91,322	notes
January 1, 2016	#5 **Stanford**	45 #6 Iowa	16 94,268	notes
January 2, 2017	#9 **USC**	52 #5 Penn State	49 95,128	notes
January 1, 2018[e]	#2 Oklahoma	48 #3 **Georgia**	54 92,844	notes
January 1, 2019	#9 Washington	23 #5 **Ohio State**	28 91,853	notes
January 1, 2020	#7 **Oregon**	28 #11 Wisconsin	27 90,462	notes
January 1, 2021[e]	#1 **Alabama**	31 #4 Notre Dame	14 18,373[b]	notes

Source:[61]

1. ^ Jump up to: ᵃ ᵇ The 1942 game was played in Duke Stadium in Durham, North Carolina, because of a restriction on crowds allowed on the West Coast after the attack on Pearl Harbor.
2. ^ Jump up to: ᵃ ᵇ The 2021 game was moved to Arlington, Texas, shortly after event organizers were unable to receive an exception from the state of California to allow fan attendance during the COVID-19 pandemic.[1]
3. ^ Jump up to: ᵃ ᵇ During World War I, military teams played
4. ^ Jump up to: ᵃ ᵇ Denotes BCS National Championship Game
5. ^ Jump up to: ᵃ ᵇ ᶜ Denotes College Football Playoff semifinal game

Was Fritz Pollard an All-American football player?

First Black All-American Football Player named to Walter Camp's team

Fritz Pollard became the first black running back from Brown University to be named to Walter Camp's All-America team. The porters refused to serve him on the team's train trip to California because he was a black man. This was a great honor because no African American player had made the Walter Camp team. Alabama Wide Receiver DeVonta Smith is the 2020 Walter Camp Player of the Year. He is the third Alabama player to win the prestigious honor, joining quarterback Tua Tagovailoa (2018) and running back Derrick henry (2015). This is why it is so important to tell the compelling story of Fritz Pollard.

I cannot imagine what it would feel like for other players than Smith, Tagovailoa and Henry to know that their name is associated with the first African American to be named to the Walter Camp All-American team. The award now has a different feeling with knowing the education around it and the impact that it will have on our sports fan and the athletes that play the game of football.

Who was Walter Camp? Walter Camp was born on April 7, 1859, in New Britain, Connecticut. His father's name was Leverett Camp. His mother's name was Ellen Sophia Cornell. Camp went to Hopkins Grammar School in New Haven, Connecticut. In 1875, he started at Yale College and graduated in 1880.

Walter Camp is recognized as one of American football's most accomplished people. He played and coached football at Yale College. Camp coached at Yale in 1888, 1891, and 1892, the teams from these years have been accepted as national champions. Camp coached and won 67 games and only lost two games. In 1951, Camp was inducted into the College Football Hall of Fame. Camp would establish the All American college football team each year. Before he passed away, Camp had written over 249 magazine articles and approximately 30 books about the game of football. Walter Camp was known as the "Father of American Football. His below quote is his opinion of Fritz Pollard.

He is one of the greatest runners I have seen
–Walter Camp

Who was the first black head coach in the NFL?

First Black NFL (National Football League) Coach

In 921, Fritz Pollard became the Head Coach of the Akron Pros and still playing running back. This would make him the First Black Coach in the NFL (National Football League). He paved the way for coaches such as Tony Dungy. Dungy was the first black head coach to win a SuperBowl when his team Indianapolis Colts defeated the Chicago Bears in Super Bowl XLI.

Tony Dungy was a player and later a coach. He went undrafted in the 1977 NFL Draft and was later signed as a free agent by the Pittsburgh Steelers of the National Football League as a safety. Dungy played on the 1978 Super Bowl Championship team with the Pittsburgh Steelers. I admire Tony Dungy because he did the same thing that Fritz Pollard did by giving black mens an opportunity to make their dreams come true. The goal is to open up the door to African Americans to take on more leadership roles in the NFL. We can talk about the black coaches in the NFL, Tony Dungy, Mike Tomlin, Art Shell and the belated, Dennis Green. The list can go on and on but Tony Dungy had that same vision as Fritz Pollard. Dungy would not take credit for being the First Black Coach in the NFL because of his intergity and the passionate way that he spoke about the man they called Fritz Pollard.

On September 30, 2002, which is my mother birthday. The late Johnnie L. Cochran, Jr. And Cyrus Mehri issued a ground-breaking report revealing that black NFL head coaches are held to a higher standard than their white counterparts. I think about Fritz Pollard and all of his accomplishment back in the

1920. He did these things with being denied to eat in the same restaurants with his white teammates or drink from the same water fountain. His vision was that we inspire others to be great and educate them on their path or juorney to build their own legacy. We are all looking for the right answer to close the gap between wrong and right but it starts with everyone reading more about the pioneers of the NFL who came before us. It is only forgotten history if we don't read. If we don't read than there you go we will never learn about these great and compelling stories of the late greats of the NFL. Firtz Pollard was the first black coach in the NFL at the age of 27 years old.

Did Akron Legend Fritz Pollard win a World championship in football?

Frederick Douglass Fritz Pollard grew up in Chicago. He was a talented baseball player and three-time Cook County track champion by the time he graduated from high school. Fritz Pollard played football for Northwestern, Dartmouth and Havard before receiving a scholarship in 1915 to attend Brown University. In 1920, Fritz Pollard opened the doors for every black athlète and minorties in the NFL. He signed a contract to play for the Akron Pros in the American Professional Football Association and guided Akron to a championship in 1920.

We have a kid from Rogers Park that was more proud of being the First Black Head Coach in the NFL than winning a World Championship. In 1886, The Pollard family moved to the small village of Rogers Park to escape racial tension in Missouri. They were a black family living in a white neighborhood in Rogers Park. He was the first African-American in a backfield position to be named and All-American college football player, and later became the first black man to play in the Bowl. Fritz Pollard son, Fritz Pollard Jr., went on to become a track and field star at Senn High School before competing in and winning a bronze medal in the 1936 Olympics in Berlin, Germany. James Cleveland Jesse Owens was at the event and won four goal medals for the United States. Mack Robinson was there too the older brother of Baseball Hall of Fame member Jackie Robinson. Mack is best known for winning a silver medal in the 1936 Summer Olympics, where he broke the Olympic Record in the 200 meter but still finished behind Jesse Owens.

Fritz spoke in interviews of his passion of being an NFL Head Coach more than anything else. Fritz Pollard was one of the first black players in the National Football League to win a World Championsihip.

Frederick Douglass Fritz Pollard Accomplishment and Timeline

The below list is just some of the legendary Fritz
Pollard achievements of the first things that he had
accomplished in his lifetime. There are so many other
things that are not listed so if you go out and read about
his life story you will be inspired as I am today.

1916: Fritz Pollard was the first African-American from Brown University to play in the Rose Bowl

1920: Fritz Pollard was the first African-American to play professional football with the Akron Pros, In 1920, The team would go on and win the World Championship in football.

1920: Fritz Pollard and Bobby Marshall were the first two African American players in the NFL in 1920.

1921: Fritz Pollard achieved one of the greatest honor that any black man could wish to be. He became the co-head coach of the Akron Pros, while still paying running back for the team that he was coaching.

1922: Fritz Pollard signed a contract with the Milwaukee Badgers. Milwaukee Badgers was a professional American football team, based in Milwaukee, Wisconsin, that played in the National Football League from 1922 to 1926. The Milwaukee team was claimed by the Green Bay Packers and they still reserve two games a season for their old Milwaukee ticket holders, and their radio station as well. He founded F.D. Pollard and Co. investment firm in 1922.

1923: Fritz Pollard was the first black quarterback on an NFL team. He was head coach for the Hammond Pros. Fritz Pollard was inducted into Hammond Pros Hall of Famers in 2005, which inducted George Papa Bear Halas in 1963. The Hammond Pros from Hammond,

Indiana played in the National Football League form 1920 to 1926 as a traveling team.

1928: Fritz Pollard established The Chicago Black Hawks (American Football) an all African-American professional football team. Fritz Pollard was the team's owner, coach, quarterback and running back. The team played most of its games on the road due to the country's economic situation and poor fans attendance. The team was disbanded three years later in 1932.

1935: Fritz Pollard coached all-black team in New York (Brown Bombers) from 1935-1938. He also founded the first black tabloid, the New York Independent News.

1954: Fritz Pollard was inducted into College Hall of Fame. His sister Noami Pollard became the first African American woman to graduate from Northwestern, His brother Leslie Pollard was on the 1908 Darmount football team.

1956: Fritz Pollard produced Rockin the Blues which included such performers as The Wanderers, The Hurricanes, Elyce Roberts, Linda Hopkins, Pearl Woods, The Five Miller Sisters, The Harptones, and Connie Carroll.

2005: Fritz Pollard was inducted into the Pro Football Hall of Fame in 2005. He died at the age of 92 in 1986.

CHAPTER SIX

Early Years Pre-NFL

First Black 2 Times All-American Football Player

William Henry Lewis was born on November 28, 1868. Lewis began his college education at Virginia Normal and Collegiate Institute (now Virginia State University). John Mercer Langston helped Lewis transfer from Virginia Normal after one year to Amherst a college in Massachusetts. Langston was an American activist, educator, abolitionist and attorney. He became the first Black Dean of the law school at Harvard University. In addition, Langston was the first black man to represent Virginia in the U.S. House of Representatives.

William Henry Lewis graduated from Amherst. He attended Harvard Law School and played center for two years for the Crimson. Lewis was named both years as a two Times All-American making him the first black man to achieve those honors. Lewis went on with his career as being an assistant coach at Harvard University. Lewis helped coach the team to a record of 114 wins, 15 loss and 5 ties from 1895-1906. The impressive part is that this took place way back in 1895.

Lewis had much success as an assistant coach. The Crimson won back-to-back National Titles in 1898 and 1899.

The Harvard Crimson Football program is one of the oldest in the United States and world. The Crimson has an legacy that includes 13 National Championships and 20 College Football Hall of Fame inductees, including the First African American college football player William Henry Lewis. In 1911, Lewis became one of the first African Americans to be recognized and admitted to the American Bar Association. The ABA (American Bar Association) was founded on August 21, 1878. This is one of the highest honor any black man can receive. President Theodore Roosevelt appointed William Henry Lewis to become the First African American Assistant U.S. Attorney. Lewis was inducted into the Virginia Sports Hall of Fame in 1980 and the College Football Hall of Fame in 2009. Lewis passed away in Boston, Massachusetts at the age of 80 in 1949.

32nd U. S. President <u>Theodore Roosevelt</u>, He was a Harvard football fan and a friend of William Henry Lewis. Roosevelt was an Harvard alumnus and invited Lewis to his estate at Oyster Bay, New York in 1900. The United States Attorney for Boston Henry P. Moulton, at the direction of Roosevelt, appointed Lewis as an Assistant United States Attorney in Boston. William Henry Lewis was the first African American to be an Assistant US Attorney in 1903.

The only limit to our realization of tomorrow will be our doubts of today. Let us move forward with strong and active faith.
-Theodore Roosevelt

The Southern white delegates said they did not know William Henry Lewis was a Negro until he entered the convention hall. The delegates wanted Lewis to resign but he refused. Attorney General <u>George W. Wickersham</u> sent a "spirited letter" to all 4,700 members of the ABA (American Bar Association) to stop the removal of William Henry Lewis.

Julia Ward Howe was an American poet and author, known for writing "The Battle Hymn of the Republic" and the original 1870 pacifist Mother's Day Proclamation. Julie was a social activist, advocate for abolitionism and had a desire to make changes in society with women's suffrage. She met the great Charles Dickens because of her father's status as a successful banker. William Henry Lewis was one of the three persons invited to deliver a speech at Boston's Symphony Hall memorial to abolitionist Julia Ward following her death in 1910.

CHAPTER SEVEN

Early Years Pre-NFL

Robert Wells Marshall was born on March 12, 1880 in Milwaukee, Wisconsin. Marshall was the son of Richard Marshall and Symanthia Gillespie Marshall. His aunt was Jessie Gillespie Herndon, the second wife of Alonzo Herndon, founder and president of the Atlanta Life Insurance Company, one of the most successful black-owned insurance business in the country. His grandfather was Ezekiel Gillespie, a former slave and civil right pioneer. He purchased his own freedom for $800. While in high school, Marshall mother died, and he began working to help support his three siblings.

Marshall competed in ice hockey, wrestling, boxing, track, baseball, however, he was best known for playing football and being one of the first to do it in the NFL. Marshall played baseball as a first baseman for three at Minneapolis Central High School. Central High was the champion for both his senior and junior years, of 1900 and 1901. Central High school was located in Minneapolis, Minnesota. The school was founded in 1860 and closed in 1982. The school colors were red and blue. Bobby played baseball for the University of Minnesota. He helped the University of Minnesota win the Western Conference Championship in 1905. He played defensive end for the football team of the University of Minnesota from 1904 to 1906. In 1906, the field goals counted as four points. Marshall kicked a 48-yard field goal to beat the University of Chicago 4-2 and being one of the first black kickers to do that. He was one of the first African American to play football in the Western Conference (later the Big Ten). Bobby Marshall graduated in 1907 and played with Minneapolis pro teams, the Marines and Deans. Marshall played from 1920 through 1924 in the National Football League with the Rock Island Independents. The Rock Island Independents were a professional American football team, based in Rock Island, Illinois, from 1907 through 1926. The team were a founding National Football League franchise. They hosted what has been called the First National Football League Game on September 26, 1920 at Douglas Park. Marshall played with the Minneapolis Marines. The Minneapolis Marines were an early professional football team that existed from 1905 until 1924. In additional, Bobby Marshall played for the Duluth Eskimos. The Duluth Eskimos were a professional team from Duluth, Minnesota in the National Football League (NFL). The team withdrew from the league after the 1927 season. The Duluth Eskimos were one of the first NFL teams to use a logo. For years, Marshall coached youngsters in boxing and football in Minneapolis. He was inducted into the College Hall of Fame in 1971. Marshall died of Alzheimer's disease in 1958.

Bobby Marshall

CHAPTER EIGHT

Early Years Pre-NFL

Paul Leroy Robeson was born on April 9, 1898 in Princeton, New Jersey. In 1915, Robeson won an academic scholarship to Rutgers College, where he was twice named a consensus All-American in football. He became the third African-American student to enroll at Rutgers and only one at a time during this era. Paul was much more than a football player. He was an lawyer, social activist, actor and singer. My favorite song that Paul sings is Ol'Man River which was inducted into the Grammy Hall of Fame. The song talks about the struggles and hardships of African Americans with uncaring, endless flowing of the Mississippi Rivera. It is sung from the point of view of a stevedore, also called a dockworker and longshoreman. A waterfront manual labor worker who is involved in loading and unloading airplanes, trains, trucks and ships. In addition, Paul was the class valedictorian meaning a student, typically having the highest academic achievements of the class, who delivers the valedictory at a graduation ceremony. Robeson was inducted into the College Football Hall of Fame in 1995. On January 23, 1976, following complications of a stroke, Paul Leroy Robeson died in Philadelphia at the age of 77.

CHAPTER NINE

Early Years Pre-NFL

Jay Williams recorded Mahalia Jackson, Muddy Waters and coached at Morehouse College

Jay Mayo "Ink" Williams was born on September 25, 1894 in Pine Bluff, Arkansas. His parents were Millie and Daniel Williams. Jay was seven years old when his father died. The family returned to Monmouth, Illinois, his mother hometown, where he grew up. William attended Brown University, where he was an exceptional football player and track star. Williams served in the U.S. Army in the First World War 1 from 1917 through 1919. Williams played professional football and one of the three black athletes (along with Paul Lewis Robeson) to play in the National Football League during its first year. He played for various teams, Canton Bulldogs, Hammond Pros, Dayton Triangles and Cleveland Bulldogs during his career from 1921 until 1926. William passion was for music even though he continued to play football. He joined Paramount Records in 1924. William was a supervisor and talent scout of recording sessions in the Chicago area, becoming the most successful "race records" producer of his time, breaking all previous records for sales in this genre.

Williams recorded Tampa Red, Jimmy Blythe, Freddy Keppard, Jelly Roll Morton, King Oliver, Ida Cox, Thomas A. Dorsey and Blind Lemon Jefferson. The singers, Ma Rainey and Papa Charlie Jackson, was his two biggest discoveries as a recording artist. William left Paramount in 1927, and started The Chicago Record Company, releasing gospel, jazz and blues records on the "Black Patti" label. Black Patti soon failed, Williams moved back to Brunswick Records. The Wall Street took a hard crash in 1929. Record sales was at an all-time low and caused many people to be out of a job including Williams. Williams left to go coach at Morehouse College in Atlanta.

In 934, Williams was hired as head of the race records department at Decca, where he recorded the great singer, Mahalia Jackson. After leaving Decca in 1945, William worked self-employed and ran several small, independent labels. From 1945 through 1949, he managed the Harlem label (based in New York City), and the Southern, Chicago, and Ebony label (based in Chicago), one of the artists he recorded was the young Muddy Waters. He earned the nickname "Ink" by his ability to get signatures of talented African-American musicians on recording contracts. Williams died on January 2, 1980 in a Chicago nursing home.

CHAPTER TEN

First Black Lineman in League History

Frederick Wayman "Duke" Slater was a judge and American football player. He was named to the Pro Football Hall of Fame's Centennial Class in 2020. He was enshrined in the College Football Hall of Fame in 1951. Frederick Slater played college football at the University of Iowa from 1918 to 1921. He was a first team All-American in 1921 playing the tackle position on the front line. Slater was a member of the Hawkeye's 1921 National Championship team. Slater was the first black lineman in league history after joining the NFL. He played 10 seasons in the NFL for the Chicago Cardinals and the Rock Island Independents, earning seven all-pro selections.

Fred Slater was born in Normal, Illinois in 1898. His father, George Slater was a Methodist minister. The family dog was named Duke, he somehow picked up name as a personal nickname, and it would stick with him for the rest of his life. The family moved to Clinton, Iowa after he turned 13 years old. His father became pastor of the A.M. E. church in Clinton. His dad was against him trying out for the football team at Clinton High School. Duke Slater was brokenhearted and went on a hunger strike for seven days, and his father finally gave in to let him try out for the team. The high school players needed to provide their own helmet and shoes. His father could not afford both, so he asked Duke to choose. He played every game at Clinton High School without a helmet. His feet were so big that his shoes had to be special ordered from Chicago. He played football for three seasons from 1913-1915 at Clinton High School. The school compiled a 22-3-1 record in Duke's three years. Clinton High School won two Iowa State Championship in 1913 and 1914. Slater scored six touchdowns from the fullback position and led the team in scoring his senior year in 1915.

CHAPTER ELEVEN

Sol Butler bough Jack's Café, preciously owned by Jack Johnson, former heavyweight champion in 1932.

Solomon W. Butler was born in Kingfisher, Oklahoma, the youngest child of Mary and Ben Butler. His mother was born in Georgia in 1867. His father was from Morgan County, Alabama, and born a slave in 1842. His father fought in the Civil War under General Butler whom he admired and took his last name. The Butler Family settled in Wichita, Kansas after escaping slavery. Sol (as he was known) made the varsity football team as a starting halfback his freshman year. He lead the school in track and field and football his freshman year. His sophomore year, He set a state record in the 100-yard dash after helping Hutchinson finish as state runner-up. In 1913, he won six firsts, broke five meet records and unofficially broke a world record in the 50-yard dash as a junior at Hutchinson High School in Kansas at the district meet. He followed his older brother to Rock Island High School in Rock Island, Illinois, his senior year in 1914. He competed against 300 of the best track stars of the Midwest in Chicago. He placed in the broad jump, 440-yard dash and 60-yard dash and hurdles. Sol broke one meet record, tied a world record, and won fourth place overall, competing against and entire track team.

Butler earned 12 varsity letters competing in baseball, football, track and field at the University of Dubuque from 1915 to 1919. He entered the military as a solider in World War 1 and represented the U.S. Army in the Inter −Allied Games in Paris, where he won the long jump. He won the U.S. National Amateur Union championship that same year by jumping 24 feet 8 inches. In 1923, he signed with the NFL team the Rock Island Independents, which local accounts raved about his first appearance in the victory over the Chicago Bears. Hammond Pros bought out his contract from the Rock Island in November 1923 for $10,000. He played for Kansas City Monarchs in 1925. He played alongside Jim Thorpe of the Canton Bulldogs where he was named starting quarterback in 1926. The New York Giants refused to play the game until Canton withdraw Butler as starting quarterback in 1926.

In 1927, Butler returned to Chicago to marry a native Kansan woman by the name of Berenice. Butler went on to work as recreation director of Chicago's Washington Park. Butler worked part-time as a probationary officer, and became sports editor for the Chicago Bee and The Defender newspaper in Chicago. His wife died before they could have any children. He spent his time after helping the youth in city parks activities within the Chicago area. He found a basketball team (Chicago All-Stars) while playing in California and decided to stay in the state. Butler used his money to purchase Jack's Café, previously owned by Jack Johnson, former heavyweight boxing champion in 1932. Butler also owned nightclubs in Chicago, set up his own talent agency and for a brief period was in record business representing Paul Robeson. Butler died on December 1, 1954, in Paddy's Liquors, a Chicago tavern where he was employed for seven years. He is buried next to his sister, Josephine Butler, at Maple Grove Cemetery in Wichita, Kansas.

CHAPTER TWELVE

First African-American to play at the historic Orange Bowl Stadium

Harold Bradley Jr. was born in Chicago, grew up in the Southside West Woodlawn neighborhood in Chicago. His father, Harold Bradley Sr., played for the Chicago Cardinals in 1928, and was one of the 13 African-Americans to participate in the NFL before World War II. Harold Bradley Jr. followed his father footsteps and played football at Englewood High School in Chicago and enrolled at the University of Iowa after graduating from high school. Harold Bradley Jr. completed the first African-American father-son combination to play football for the Hawkeyes in 1926. Bradley Jr. was one of five African-Americans to play for the Hawkeye football team in 1950, when the team finished the season with a road game at the University of Miami. Bradley and his four African-American teammates, nicknamed the **"Orange Bowl Five"** became the first-African-Americans to play at the historic Orange Bowl stadium, a contest won by Miami, 14-6.

Bradley served for three years in the U.S. Marines after leaving Iowa. He played football for a team called the Marines Corps Recruit Depot San Diego Devil Dog from 1951-1953, where he was discovered by a coach for the Cleveland Browns. He played three seasons for the Cleveland Browns from 1954-1956, winning NFL championship with the team in 1954 and 1955. Bradley finished his professional football career with the Philadelphia Eagles in 1958. Bradley joined with his father to complete the first African-American father-son combination to ever play in the NFL in 1950.

CHAPTER THIRTEEN

The Midnight Express "The name given by the Media"

Joseph Johnny Lillard Jr., was born in Tulsa, Oklahoma to Annie Johnson and Joe Lillard. He was the first of the couple two children. At the early age of six, he took up baseball, and some of his other hobbies were tap dancing and singing. Lillard was nine years old when his mother died, and his father had been away from home about six years before that time. He moved to Mason City, Iowa with his relatives in 1915. Lillard attended Mason City High School, where he won all-state honors, and claimed several Iowa track titles. After high school, He was planning on attending the University of Minnesota, once he found out that his coach, Clarence Spears was going to the University of Oregon. He had a change of mind. Lillard decided to follow his coach to go to college at Oregon. He played on the school freshman team his first year. The following year, Lillard appeared in two games for the varsity team. He was responsible for all points in a 9-0 Ducks win over Idaho. Lillard was suspended by the PCC before Oregon's next game. He was suspended due to breaking college amateurism rules by playing semi-professional baseball for the Gilkerson Colored Giants.

The violation placed Lillard's college eligibility in question. Lillard claimed that he received money not for playing, but for driving the team. He did play in games. The decision was overturned, according to PCC rules, no protest was going on during the week prior to a game between PCC teams. The Ducks claimed an upset victory, 13-0 in the second game of the season against Washington. Lillard had two interception and a touchdown in the game. Lillard dropped out of the university after long going issues with the PCC decision. After the end of his college career, Lillard participated in a professional all-star game on November 26, 1931. He had a 55-yard touchdown run that helped his team win the first all-star game. The second all-star game was no different; he recorded a 45-yard touchdown run for a Chicago-based team in a 20-6 win. These highlights attracted the attention of the NFL teams. He joined the Chicago Cardinals for the 1932 NFL season. Lilliard performances in his first and second NFL games was praised by the Chicago Defender, which called him "the whole show."

During his time in the NFL, he was regard as a player with the ability to many things on the football field. He could pass, catch, run and kick. Lilliard received racial abuse from fans but keep on playing the game of football that he loved. After his NFL career ended, Lillard joined the Westwood Cubs of Pacific Coast Football League in 1934. He threw for the most touchdowns than any player in the league and ran for the second most touchdowns. In 1935, He drew interest from coach Fritz Pollard, who was coaching for the New York Brown Bombers. Lillard was the 12th black player in the history of the NFL. He was the lone African-American playing in the 132 and one of two in 1933, the other was Ray Kemp, a tackle with the Pirates.

CHAPTER FOURTEEN

Honoring the Pittsburgh Steeler Logo
(AISI) and steel mill workers.

The material used to make steel, Yellow for Coal, Orange for iron ore and blue for steel scraps.

Ray Kemp was born on April 7, 1907, in the small township of Cecil, Pennsylvania. The city is located in Washington County in the state of Pennsylvania. He was an African-American football player and a charter member of the Pittsburgh Pirates football team (now called the Pittsburgh Steelers). The Steel Curtain was later one of the most popular name. The Steel Curtain was one of the toughest defensive line of the 1970s American football team of the NFL. The defense allowed an average 3.1 points per game and the team had an average margin victory of 22 points. The four members of the Steel Curtains were: #63-Ernie "Fats" Holmes, #78-Dwight "Mad Dog" White, #68- L.C. "Hollywood Bags" Greenwood, and #75, Mean Joe Greene. Do you remember the kid asking Mean Joe Greene in the coke commercial if he needed help? I wish I could have been that kid that caught Mean Joe Greene game jersey. Why is the Ray Kemp story important?

In 1933, Raymond Howard Kemp was the only African-American on the team and only one of two black players in the entire National Football League. Ray Kemp graduated from Cecil High School in 1926. The 1920s were groundbreaking moments for African-American players in the National Football League. After graduating from high school, Kemp worked in the coal mines around Cecil, Pennsylvania for one year before enrolling at Duquesne University. Coal mining was not an easy job and required digging and extracting coal from the ground. He was coached by Elmer Layden, a former member of Notre Dame's Legendary Four Horsemen (Jim Crowley, Don Miller, Harry Stuhldreher and Elmer Layden) who were the backfield of Notre Dame's 1924-football team under coach Knute Rockne. Layden was the commissioner of the National Football League from 1941 to 1946.

Ray Kemp became a starter for the Duquesne Dukes during his sophomore year and by the end of his senior year season, he received honorable mention on the All-American list. Kemp finished college and future Pirates owner, Art Rooney, told Kemp that he would like him to play for his "J. P. semi-pro team". In 1932, Kemp played for two semi-pro teams, J.P. Rooney's and Ernie Pros in his spare time. J.P. Rooneys became the NFL's Pittsburg Pirates the following year. Kemp joined the team and became one of only two black players in the league, the other being Joe Lillard of the Chicago Cardinals. Kemp was cut by the team after playing in three games against, the Boston Redskins, New York Giants and Chicago Cardinals. Kemp appealed the cut but Rooney refused to go over the head coach, Forrest McCreery "Jap Douds", who was a player-coach, also played the same position as Kemp. In 1933, Jap Douds became the first coach of the Pittsburgh Steelers.

Kemp went back to his old job at the steel mill and the Pirates went 2-5 over the next seven games. He was requested back by the team and with only two days of practice played the entire game at tackle against the New York Giants, who would defeat the Pirates 27-3 at the Polo Grounds. The Polo Grounds was the name of three stadiums in Upper Manhattan, New York City, used mainly for professional baseball and American football from 1880 through 1963. Kemp was asked to leave the hotel the Friday before the New York game. Kemp refused and the Giants game would be his final game in the NFL. The next season, he was hired as the head football coach at Bluefield State College. Bluefield State College is a historically black college in Bluefield, West Virginia. It is a member school of the Thurgood Marshall College Fund.

The NFL would not have any black players with the exist of Kemp of Lillard until the arrival of Kenny Washington in 1946.

The first African –American to sign a contract with a National Football League (NFL) team in the modern (post-World War II) era.

Kenny S. Washington was born in Los Angeles, California. He grew up in Lincoln Heights one of the oldest neighborhoods in Los Angeles, California. His father was Edgar "Blue" Washington an American actor and professional baseball player. Edgar appeared in 74 films between 1919 and 1957, and was given the nickname "Blue" by film director Frank Capra. Edgar played in the Negro Leagues for a few years as a pitcher for the Los Angeles White Sox and the Chicago American Giants, and played first baseman for the Kansas City Monarchs. Kenny was raised by his grandmother Susie and his uncle Rocky, the first black uniformed lieutenant watch commander in the Los Angeles Police Department (LAPD). He was a star at both football and baseball at Abraham Lincoln High School, where he was nicknamed "Kingfish" after a character in the radio show Amos 'n' Andy. Washington led both teams to city championships in the same calendar year. The high school is named after Abraham Lincoln, the 16th President of the United States. Kenny Washington attended the University of California, Los Angeles (UCLA), where was a member of both the football and Bruins baseball team. Washington was graded better than his teammate, the legendary Jackie Robinson as a baseball player. Four Times- World Series Champion, Brooklyn Dodgers manager, Leo Durocher wanted to offer Washington a contract to play for the team but he would have to travel to Puerto Rico as part of the deal. The story goes that Washington refused the agreement. Washington rushed for 1,914 yards in his college career, a school record for 34 years. He was one of four African-Americans players on the 1939 Bruins football team, the others being Ray Bartlett, Robinson, and Woody Strode. This was not a known factor to have four black players on the same team when only a few dozen played on college football teams.

In 1939, Washington was the first Bruin to lead the nation in total offense and became the first consensus All-American in the history of the school's football program. He was named to second-team All-America selection instead of the first and was omitted from the East-West Shrine Bowl Game that year. Teams consist of players from colleges in the Eastern United States vs. The Western United States. The game's logo, featuring a young girl recovering from surgery walking with Boston College Eagles player Mike Esposito before the 1974 game. His teammates have commented how strong Washington was when confronted with racial slurs and discrimination so there were outrage with the media with this decision. Washington coached football at UCLA and joined the LAPD. Washington played for the Hollywood Bears of the Pacific Coast Professional Football League from 1940 to 1945. He was the league's highest paid player. George Halas "Papa Bear", owner of the Chicago Bears tried to convince the league to permit integration but was not successful. Washington earned recognition each year and even when he suffered a knee injury that prevented him being recruited to the war. In 1945, Washington did serve in the USO (United States Organizations) tour as a type of sports representative, visiting troops and playing in exhibition games. The Cleveland Rams moved to Los Angeles. The Los Angeles Ram signed Kenny Washington on March 21, 1946, followed by Woody Strode on May 7, 1946. Washington underwent surgery in both knees (his fifth surgery overall–as a child he contracted rickets (a condition that results in weak or soft bones in children) and he was once hit by a car. This all happened prior to his first NFL season. He played for the Rams for three years. In 1948, Washington retired and 80,000 people attended his final game and the entire stadium gave him a standing ovation. Washington died of heart and lung problems at the the age of 52 in Los Angeles, California.

Special Players

Jim Brown –No. 32

Position: Fullback

High School: Manhasset (Manhasset, New York)

College: University of Syracuse (Syracuse Orange retires No. 44)

NFL Draft: 1957/Round 1/Pick: 6

NFL Team: Cleveland Brown (1957–1965)–NFL Champion (1964) and 3x NFL Most Valuable Player (1957, 1958, 1965) Cleveland Brown retires No. 32

Special Players

John B. Wooten–No. 60 and 67

Position: Guard

High School: Carlsbad (NM)

College: Colorado

NFL Draft: 1959 /Round: 5/ Pick: 53

NFL Teams: Cleveland Brown (1959-1967) Washington Redskins (1968).

Special Players

Jerry Rice-No. 80

Position: Wide Receiver

High School: Moor (Oktoc, Mississippi)

College: Mississippi Valley State

NFL Draft: 1985 /Round: 1/ Pick: 6

NFL Teams: San Francisco 49ers (1985-2000)-(3x Super Bowl Champion, XXIII, XXIV, XXIX) Super Bowl MVP (XXIII) - Oakland Raiders (2001-2004), Seattle Seahawks (2004) and Denver Broncos (2005).

Special Players

Earl Christy-No. 45

Position: Running Back, Defensive Back,
Kick off, and punt return specialist

High School: Havre de Grace High School in Maryland

College: Maryland State College (MSC)

NFL Draft: The New York Jets signed Earl Christy in 1966.

NFL Team: New York Jets (1966-1969), AFL
Champion (1969) and Super Bowl Champion (III)

Special Players

Billy Joe- No. 18, 3, 33, 35

Position: Running Back

College: Villanova

NFL Draft: 1963/Round: 9/Pick: 119

AFL Draft: 1963/Round: 11/Pick: 85

NFL Teams: Denver Broncos (1963-1964) Buffalo Bills (1965) Miami Dolphins (1966) New York Jets (1967-1969) played on the 1968 Super Bowl team. Earl Christy was his roommate.

Coach: Billy Joe was Miles College (Head Football Coach) from (2008-2010).

Special Players

Ray Lewis-No. 52

Position: Middle Linebacker

High School: Kathleen (Lakeland, Florida)

College: University of Miami

NFL Draft: 1996/Round: 1/Pick: 6

NFL Team: Baltimore Ravens (1996-2012)-2x Super Bowl Champion (XXXV, XLVII) and Super Bowl MVP (XXXV)

Special Players

Tony Dorsett-No. 33

Position: Running Back

High School: Aliquippa (PA) Hopewell

College: Pittsburg (National Champion
and Heisman Trophy 1976)

NFL Draft: 1977/Round: 1/Pick: 2

NFL Teams: Dallas Cowboys (1977-1987)-Super
Bowl Champion (XII) and Denver Broncos (1988)

Special Players

Emmitt Smith–No. 22

Position: Running Back

High School: Escambia (Pensacola, Florida)

College: University of Florida –Heisman Trophy finalist and SEC Most Valuable Player (1989)

NFL Teams: Dallas Cowboys (1990–2002)–3x Super Bowl Champion (XXVII, XXVIII, XXX), Super Bowl MVP (XXVIII) and Arizona Cardinals (2003-2004)

Special Players

Gary Burley founded Pro Start Academy to help mentor young athletes to give them a competitive advantage by building a bridge to success on and off the field of play for student-athletes."

Gary Burley–No. 67

Position: Defensive Lineman

High School: Grove City High (Grove City, Ohio)

College: Pittsburg

NFL Draft: 1975/Round: 3/Pick: 55

NFL Teams: Cincinnati Bengals (1976–1983) and Atlanta Falcons (1984)

Special Players

Archie Griffin-No. 45

Position: Running back

High School: Eastmoor (Columbus, Ohio)

College: Ohio State-2x Heisman Trophy (1974, 1975) The First African-American and only player in College history to win the Heisman twice. The award was first given in 1935 to Jay Berwanger. In 1936, John Heisman died and the trophy was renamed in his honor. Ohio State retires Archie Griffin #45.

NFL Draft: 1976/Round: 1/Pick: 24

NFL Team: Cincinnati Bengals (1976-1982)

United States Football League (USFL)
Team: Jacksonville Bulls

Special Players

Alan Page-No. 88

Position: Defensive tackle

High School: Canton Central Catholic High School

College: University of Notre Dame (2x National Champion 1964 and 1966) and University of Minnesota Law School

NFL/AFL Draft: 1967/Round: 1/Pick: 15

NFL Teams: Minnesota Viking (1967-1978) NFL Champion (1969) NFL Most Valuable Player and Defensive Player of the Year (1971) Chicago Bears (1978-1981)

Special Players

J. C. Watts – No. 1

Position: Quarterback

High School: Eufaula Public Schools

College: University of Oklahoma

NFL Draft: Drafted by New York Jets of the National Football League. The Jets tried Watts at several positions and could not guarantee that he would play quarterback.

Canadian Football League: Ottawa Rough Riders (1981-1986) Grey Cup and Japan Bowl Most Valuable Player (1981) and Toronto Argonauts (1986)

Special Players

Ozzie Newsome –No. 82

Position: Tight End

High School: Colbert County (Leighton, Alabama)

College: University of Alabama (Nicknamed "The Wizard of Oz, Newsome never missed a game during his four years at Alabama

NFL Draft: 1978/Round: 1/Pick: 23

NFL Team: Cleveland Brown (1978-1990) as executive for Baltimore Raven -2x Super Bowl Champion (XXXV, XLVII)

Special Players

John Mitchell –No. 97

Position: Defensive End and Linebacker

High School: Williamson (Mobile, Alabama)

College: Junior College, Eastern Arizona and University of Alabama (NCAA Football National Champion (as coach)-1973 (Alabama)

NFL Draft: 1973/Round: 7/Pick: 174

NFL Team: San Francisco 49ers, and Pittsburgh Steelers (2x Super Bowl Champion XL, XLIII) as a coach.

Special Players

Reggie White–No. 92

Position: Defensive End

High School: Howard (Chattanooga Tennessee)

College: Tennessee-SEC Player of the year (1983)

Supplemental Draft: 1984/Round: 1/Pick: 4

American Football: Memphis Showboats (1984-1985)

NFL Teams: Philadelphia Eagles (1985-1992), Green Bay Packers (1993-1998) Super Bowl Champion (XXXI) 3x Defensive Player of the Year (1987, 1991, 1995) Nickname "The Minister of Defense" and Carolina Packers (2000)

Special Players

Ernie Davis –No. 44 and 45

Position: Halfback

High School: Elmira (NY) Free Academy

College: Syracuse-National Champion (1959)
The First African-American to win Heisman
Trophy (1961) Syracuse Orange retired #44

NFL Draft: 1962/Round: 1/Pick: 1

AFL Draft: 1962/Round: 1/Pick: 4

NFL Teams: Washington Redskins (1962) and
Cleveland Browns (1962) Browns retired #45

Special Players

Walter Payton–No. 34

Position: Running Back

High School: Columbia (Columbia, Mississippi)

College: Jackson State

NFL Draft: 1975/Round: 1/Pick: 4

NFL Teams: Chicago Bears (1975-1987) Super Bowl
Champion (XX) NFL Most Valuable Player, Offensive
Player of the Year and Walter Payton NFL Man of
the Year (1977) Chicago Bears retired #34

**Mike Ditka described Payton as the greatest football player
he had ever seen–but even greater as a human being**

Special Players

Eric Dickerson –No. 29

Position: Running Back

High School: Sealy High School (Sealy, Texas)

College: SMU (Mustangs of Southern Methodist University)

NFL Draft: 1983/Round: 1/Pick: 2

NFL Teams: Los Angeles Rams (1983-1987), Indianapolis Colts (1987-1991), Los Angeles Raiders (1992) and Atlanta Falcons (1993). Over the course of his career, Dickerson earned the name "Mr. Fourth Quarter" because he could turn up a notch as the others were winding down.

NFL Record: 2,105 rushing yards in a season

Special Players

Lawrence Taylor–No. 56

Position: Linebacker

High School: Lafayette High School (Williamsburg, Virginia)

College: University of North Carolina at Chapel Hill-ACC Player of the Year (1980)

NFL Draft: 1981 /Round: 1/Pick: 2

NFL Teams: New York Giants (1981-1993) 2x Super Bowl Champion (XXI, XXV) NFL Most Valuable Player (1986) 3x NFL Defensive Player of Year (1981, 1982, 1986) 2x NFC Player of the Year and nicknamed "L.T."

Special Players

Barry Sanders-No. 20

Position: Running Back

High School: Wichita North (Wichita)

College: Oklahoma State (Barry Sanders was the first Oklahoma State player to win the Heisman Trophy in 1988). Sanders broke an absurd 34 NCAA records in 1988.

NFL Draft: 1989/Round: 1/Pick: 3

NFL Teams: Detroit Lions (1989-1998) 2x NFL Offensive Player of Year (1994, 1997) NFL Offensive Rookie of the Year (1989) NFL Most Valuable Player (1997) and Detroit Lions retired #20

Special Players

First IUP (Indiana University of Pennsylvania)
player to be drafted in the NFL

Dave Smith –No. 88

Position: Wide Receiver

High School: New York (NY)

College: IUP (Waynesburg, Indiana (PA)

NFL Draft: 1970/Round: 8/Pick: 184

NFL Team: Pittsburgh Steelers (1970-1972) Houston
Oilers (1972-1972) Kansas City Chiefs (1973-1973)

Special Players

First Black Player who accepted a scholarship for the 1971 season at the University of Alabama.

Wilbur Jackson-No. 40

Position: Running Back

High School: Carroll (Ozark, Alabama)

College: University of Alabama- National Champion (1973).

NFL Draft: 1974/Round: 1/Pick: 9

NFL Teams: San Francisco 49ers (1974-1979)-(Super Bowl Champion XVII) and Jackson played for Washington Redskins (1980-1982).

Special Players

Philippians 4:13 I can do all things through
Christ who gives me strength. (KJV)

2 Timothy 1:7-For God hath not given us the spirit of fear,
but of power, and of love, and of a sound mind. (KJV)

Mark 10:27 Jesus looked at them and said, With
man this is impossible, but not with God; all
things are possible with God. (KJV)

Council Rudolph –No. 77, 74 and 78

Position: Defensive End

High School: Anniston City Schools (Anniston, Alabama)

Motto: Ensuring Excellence in All Things by Empowering
All Students to Become Life-Long Learners

College: Kentucky State

NFL Draft: 1972/Round: 7/Pick: 160

NFL Teams: Houston Oilers (1972) St. Louis Cardinals
(1973-1975) Tampa Bay Buccaneers (1976-

Special Players

Tyrone Keys–No. 98 and 93

Position: Defensive Lineman

High School: Callaway High School (Jackson, Mississippi) in the 1975 football season Callaway High won the Big East Conference State title. The 1975 Callaway team, which keys played on, was the first Big Eight team in the state of Mississippi to record a 12-0 record; it is also the last team over 50 years from the Jackson Mississippi metro area to go undefeated and rank as the No. 1 team in the state.

College: Mississippi State

NFL Draft: New York Jets 1981/Round: 5/Pick: 113

NFL Teams: BC Lions (Canadian Football League) (1981 -1982), Chicago Bears (1983-1985) Super Bowl Champions (XX) Tampa Bay Buccaneers (1986-1987) and the San Diego Chargers (1988).

The 1985 Chicago Bears was the first sport team to have their own rap video. The song "The Super Bowl Shuffle was nominated for a Grammy Award in 1985 for Best R&B Performance by a Duo or Group, eventually losing to "Kiss" by Prince. Over $300,000 in profits from the song and music video was donated to the Chicago Community Trust to help needy families in Chicago with food, shelter and clothing. This was in line with Walter Payton's rap lyrics in the song:

"Now we're not doing this because we're greedy, the Bears are doing it to feed the needy."

TYRONE KEYS SPEAKING FROM THE HEART

In 1969, The World Champions Kansas Chiefs played the Cincinnati Bengals in my hometown. A dream come true we had a chance to attend the game go to practice to get autographs from the players. It was my first time seeing black and white people having fun together. I was in astonishment having never seen this before and watching them showing brotherly love to each other. I did not want to leave and could have stayed there forever watching the unity among black and white football players who had just won the Super Bowl. Then reality hit me as the black players got on one bus and the white players got on another bus.

The Brian Song movie inspired me to want to play football for the Chicago Bears after watching it in six grade with the integration in Mississippi. The story was about Chicago Bears running back Brian Piccolo and Gale Sayers who were the first interracial roommates in the history of the NFL. The movie records the developments of their friendship from their rookie season in 1965, ending with Brian Piccolo's death in 1970. The movie is viewed as one of the greatest television film ever made, as well as one of the greatest films ever produced in the sports era. In 1971, the movie was the most watched in U.S. television history. From that moment, I knew what I wanted to be in life. I never missed a NFL Sunday evening or Monday night football game. My mother was not a fan of me staying up late and wanted me to go to bed early. My dad introduced me to football five decades ago. I never imagined this would take me on a journey that would help me open up doors for others as I walk in after them.

I have learned as being a State Champion, and a Super Bowl Champion that football without education is like having a ball with no air. I was blessed to have great coaches, teammates and to have a great example in my 6th grade teacher Mrs. Hagan who was a trailblazer and empowered every student back in those days that we are created equal and do not let anyone tell you different. Mrs. Hagan was the first white teacher to integrate with Dawson Elementary School. She stood in the middle of darkness because people in her own neighborhood did not want her to teach the black kids. Mrs. Hagan lead by example by showing compassion to help young peoples that would later on make them true champions in real life. How ironic without knowledge four decades later we would reconnect and both receive the 2010 Trail Blazer award. She received the award in Baton Rouge, Louisiana and I accepted the award in Tampa, Florida. The next year Mrs. Hagan went back to what she love doing and started teaching part-time. I surprised her by calling the school and she allowed me to speak to one of her 6th grade students who loved the Bears. I told him that I would send him a signed cap. I asked him to tell me his name, and just take one guess. You are right, it was Tyrone.

JENNIFER A. GARRETT SPEAKING FROM THE HEART

As a student athlete who is looking to succeed in both sports and academics, you must manage your time effectively. This means being intentional with how you spend every single minute, minimizing distractions and only giving your time to people who, and activities that, are propelling you forward and helping you to become better at your craft. All days matters, do not take any of them for granted. So make sure that you suit up each day with the right mindset and with purpose, and that you show up in every single moment as if you are supposed to be there. When you do this, you will always, "move the ball."

HOW DO I HELP MY DREAM OF BECOMING AN NFL PLAYER A REALITY?

First, you have to make good grades and play great sports!
It is a two-part process. Academics + Athletics!

Academics (NCAA / Core GPA)

NCAA

There are different divisions, or levels play, and different qualifications for each division.

To be eligible to play at the Division 1 Level, you must qualify through the NCAA.

You will register online at www.ncaa.org.

The registration fee is $90 USD.

If you are eligible for free or reduced lunch, the $90 fee can be waived.

The NCAA will require you to have a 2.5 Core GPA.

Your Core GPA is the GPA used in your 10-7 Qualification Period, the Fall Semester of your Senior Year.

During that period, the NCAA will calculate your GPA using your highest grades in 10 of your core classes.

Core Classes are English, Math, History and Science.

Other core classes are listed on your state's 48-H list.

These other core classes can be substituted, if taken, for core classes with lower grades.

The NCAA will require you to send an official transcript directly to their office.

The NAA will evaluate your transcript for Core Classes completed,

The address is:

NCAA Headquarters

700 W Washington St,

Indianapolis, IN 46204

How Do I Help My Dream of Becoming An NFL Player A Reality?

Student is required to take the ACT or the SAT

ACT

The highest score you can make on the ACT is 36.

You register for the ACT online at www.actstudent.org.

You are allowed to send your score to 4 college and universities for free when registering for the ACT.

You should send your score directly to the ACT as one of your school codes.

The school code for the NCAA is below:

New ACT Test Registration
Send your scores directly to the NCAA
Clearinghouse upon registration
Use SCHOOL CODE 9999

The fee for the ACT is $55 USD without writing and $70 USD with writing.

The ACT Composite score (1-36) is used for college admission.

A 19 ACT Composite will gain admission to most US colleges and universities.

The ACT score is an average of the English, Math, Reading and Science scores.

ACT Writing is not included in the ACT Composite scores.

The ACT will require an 18 English and / or a 20 Math to avoid taking Remedial Classes.

Remedial Classes re less than Freshman level classes that must be passed to earn the right to take Freshman level classes.

Remedial classes must be paid for, but do not count towards graduation or your major.

It is important to research the requirements for admission, merit-based scholarships and eligibility requirements for your college of choice.

Merit-based, or presidential scholarships, are based on your GPA and ACT/SAT score.

Remember, if you are not accepted as a student at the college or university, you cannot be a student-athlete that plays at the college or university.

How Do I Help My Dream of Becoming An NFL Player A Reality?

Try to have scored as close to a perfect ACT 36 by the end of the summer before your Senior year.

You can take the ACT 12 times in your lifetime.

You should begin taking the ACT at age 13, as you can register for the ACT online at this age.

The ACT will take the highest score of the 12 times taken to calculate your ACT SUPERSCORE!

It is to your advantage to take the ACT all 12 times, or as many times as you need to in order to be as close to an ACT 36 perfect score as possible.

All colleges and universities accept the ACT and the SAT.

You should take an ACT prep course to prepare for the ACT before taking the actual test.

If you need help with ACT prep, Calculating your Core GPA, or NCAA Clearance guidance, contact:

Ms. Valencia Belle
ACT Certified Educator
SCHOOLS / CLEARED Programs
(251) 298-7111

How Do I Help My Dream of Becoming An NFL Player A Reality?

schoolsprograms@gmail.com
www.schoolsprograms.org

Recruiting Realities by the Numbers
NCSA (Next College Student Athlete)
1,057,382
High School Players

73,063
College Football Players

6.9%
Compete in College

2.7%
Compete in D1

1.6%
Drafted by NFL

Source:
ncaa.org

CPSIA information can be obtained
at www.ICGtesting.com
Printed in the USA
BVHW070049160921
616802BV00008B/989